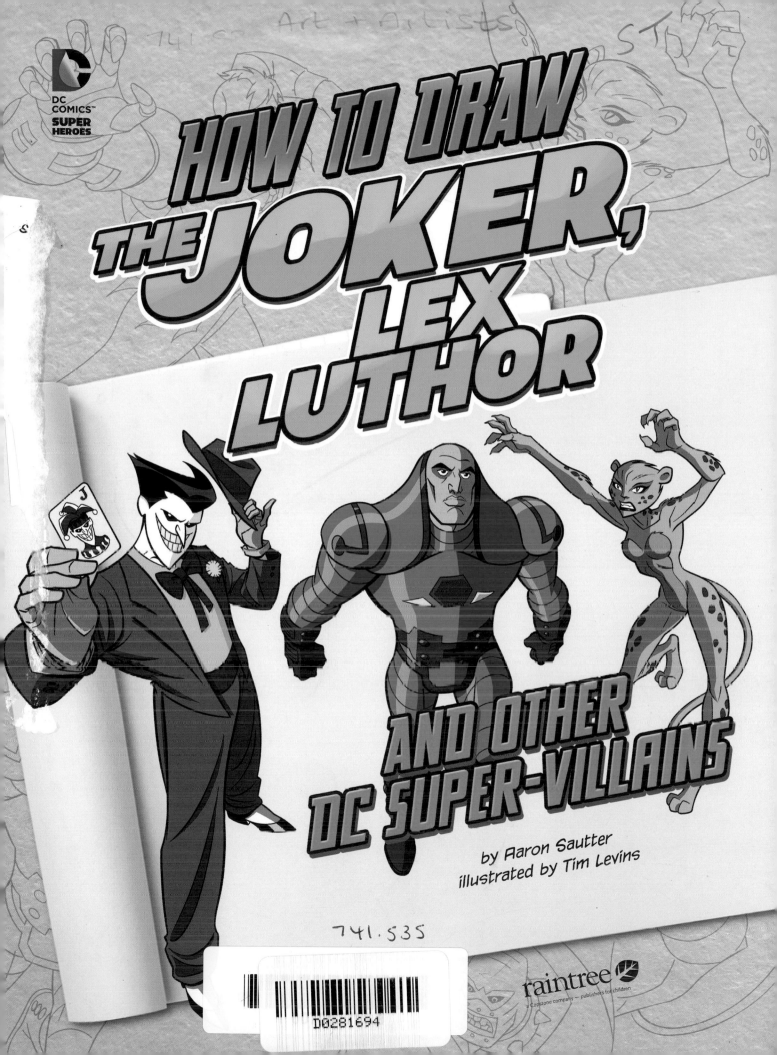

HOW TO DRAW THE JOKER, LEX LUTHOR
AND OTHER DC SUPER-VILLAINS

by Aaron Sautter

illustrated by Tim Levins

raintree
a Capstone company – publishers for children

Raintree is an imprint of Capstone Global Library Limited, a company incorporated in
England and Wales having its registered office at 7 Pilgrim Street, London, EC4V 6LB –
Registered company number: 6695582

www.raintree.co.uk
myorders@raintree.co.uk

STAR33521

Credits

Designer: Ted Williams
Art Director: Nathan Gassman
Production Specialist: Kathy McColley

ISBN 978 1 406 29194 0
18 17 16 15 14
10 9 8 7 6 5 4 3 2 1

British Library Cataloguing in Publication Data

A full catalogue record for this book is available from the British Library.

Design Elements

Capstone Studio: Karon Dubke
Shutterstock: Artishok, Bennyartist, Eliks, gst, Mazzzur, Roobcio

Printed and bound in China.

DRAWING PROJECTS

LET'S DRAW DC SUPER-VILLAINS!

What would Superman or Batman do if they didn't need to stop Lex Luthor or the Joker? How would Wonder Woman spend her time if she didn't have to fight Cheetah? Everybody loves super heroes, but the truth is — without super-villains to fight against, super heroes wouldn't have much to do.

Every super hero has a Rogues Gallery of villains to fight. Just like heroes, super-villains have a variety of powers, special abilities and backgrounds. Some are super-intelligent humans. Others are powerful aliens. Some villains devise evil plans to get revenge on their arch-enemies. Others simply want to take over and rule the world. But villains all have one thing in common — they give us a reason to cheer for our favourite super heroes!

Welcome to the world of DC super-villains! On the following pages you'll learn to draw several fearsome villains such as Sinestro, Cheetah and Black Manta.

Unleash your imagination and see what happens when your favourite heroes clash with these sinister super-villains!

WHAT YOU'LL NEED

You don't need superpowers to draw menacing villains. But you'll need some basic tools. Gather the following stationery before starting your amazing art.

PAPER: You can get special drawing paper from art and craft shops. But any type of blank, unlined paper will be fine.

PENCILS: Drawings should be done in pencil first. Even professionals use them. If you make a mistake, it'll be easy to rub out and redraw. Keep plenty of these essential drawing tools on hand.

PENCIL SHARPENER: To make clean lines, you need to keep your pencils sharp. Get a good pencil sharpener. You'll use it a lot.

ERASERS: As you draw, you're bound to make mistakes. Erasers give artists the power to turn back time and rub out those mistakes. Get some high quality rubber or kneaded erasers. They'll last a lot longer than pencil erasers.

BLACK FELT-TIP PENS: When your drawing is ready, trace over the final lines with black felt-tip pen. The dark lines will help to make your characters stand out on the page.

COLOURED PENCILS AND PENS: Ready to finish your masterpiece? Bring your characters to life and give them some colour with coloured pencils or pens.

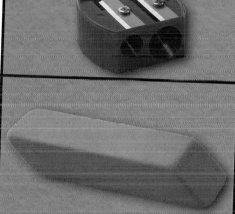

THE JOKER

Real Name: unknown

Home Base: Gotham City

Occupation: professional criminal

Enemy of: Batman

Abilities: above-average strength, genius-level intellect, skills in chemistry and engineering

Background: Also known as the Clown Prince of Crime, the Joker is Batman's most dangerous enemy. When he fell into a vat of toxic waste, he was transformed into an evil madman. The chemicals bleached his skin white, dyed his hair green and peeled his lips back into a permanent, hideous grin. The Joker delights in tormenting Batman and the innocent people of Gotham City.

DRAWING IDEA
Try drawing the Joker with a deadly hand buzzer or other practical joke device.

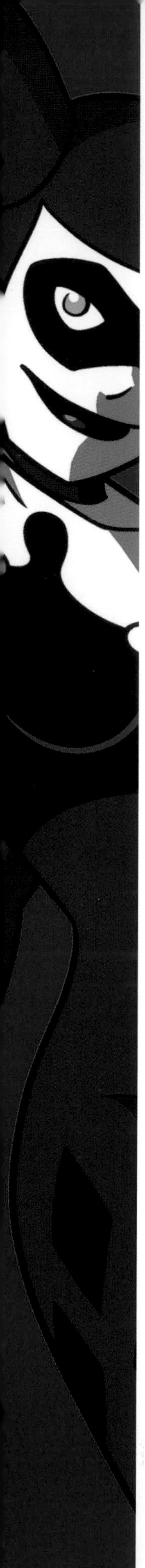

1

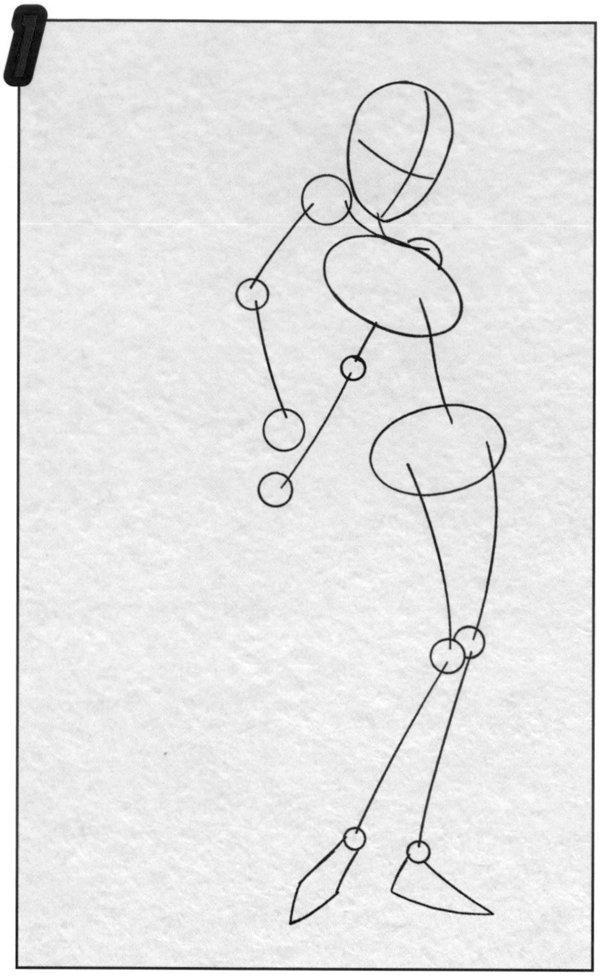

2

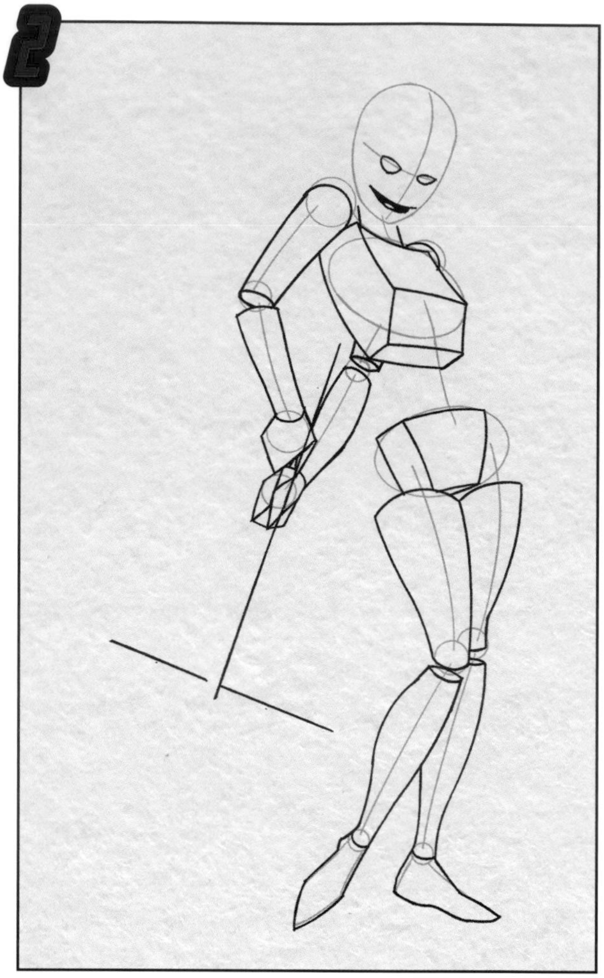

3

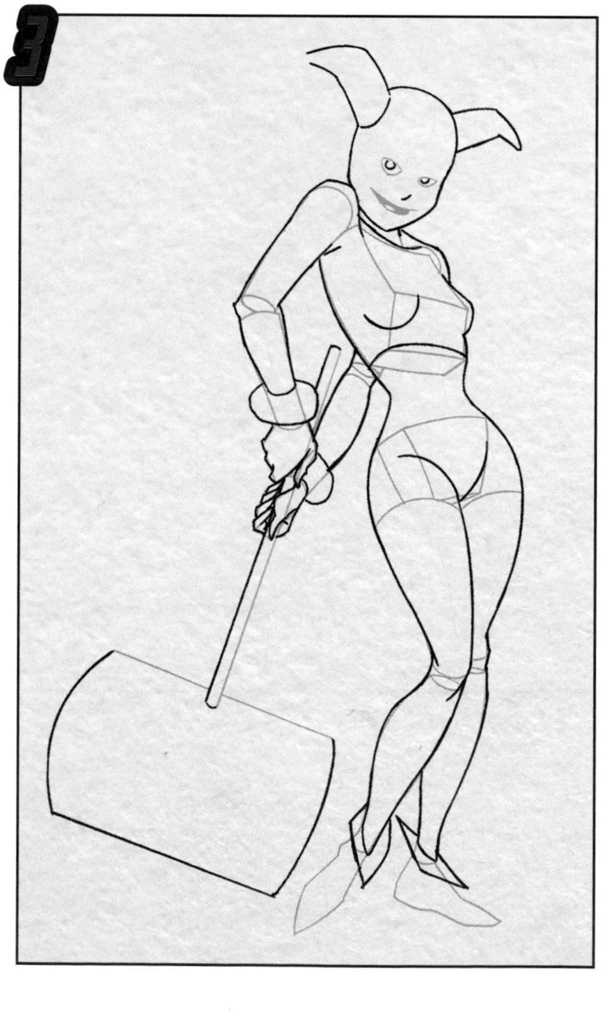

4

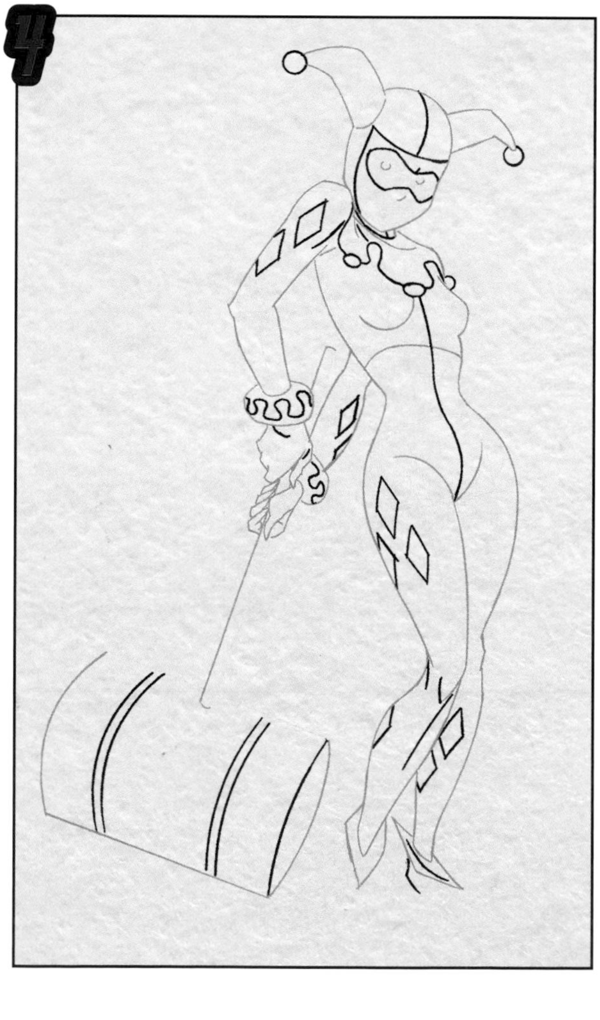

HARLEY QUINN

Real Name: Dr. Harleen Quinzel

Home Base: Gotham City

Occupation: psychiatrist, professional criminal

Enemy of: Batman

Abilities: Olympic-level gymnast and acrobat

Equipment: giant mallet

Background: Dr. Harleen Quinzel was once a successful psychiatrist at Gotham City's Arkham Asylum. But when she met the Joker everything changed. When the Joker told Harley the heartbreaking, but false, story of his troubled childhood, her heart was won over. Harley fell in love with the Joker and soon helped him to escape. She now clowns around Gotham City as Harley Quinn, the Joker's girlfriend and partner in crime.

DRAWING IDEA
Try drawing Harley and the Joker working together to set a deadly trap for Batman and Robin.

9

BANE

Real Name: unknown

Home Base: Gotham City

Occupation: assassin and professional criminal

Enemy of: Batman

Abilities: superhuman strength, genius-level intellect

Equipment: Venom drug

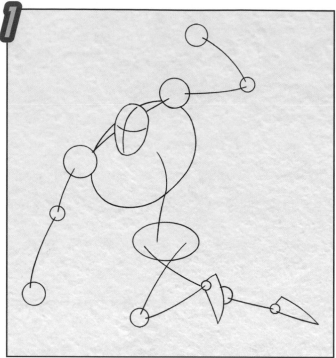

Background: Bane's background is a mystery, even to Batman. The only thing known for sure is that Bane was once a prisoner. He was chosen as a test subject for a new drug called Venom. The drug gave Bane superhuman strength. He now uses it to stay strong and works as one of Gotham City's criminal masterminds. Bane's greatest desire is to be the one person who can defeat the Dark Knight — permanently.

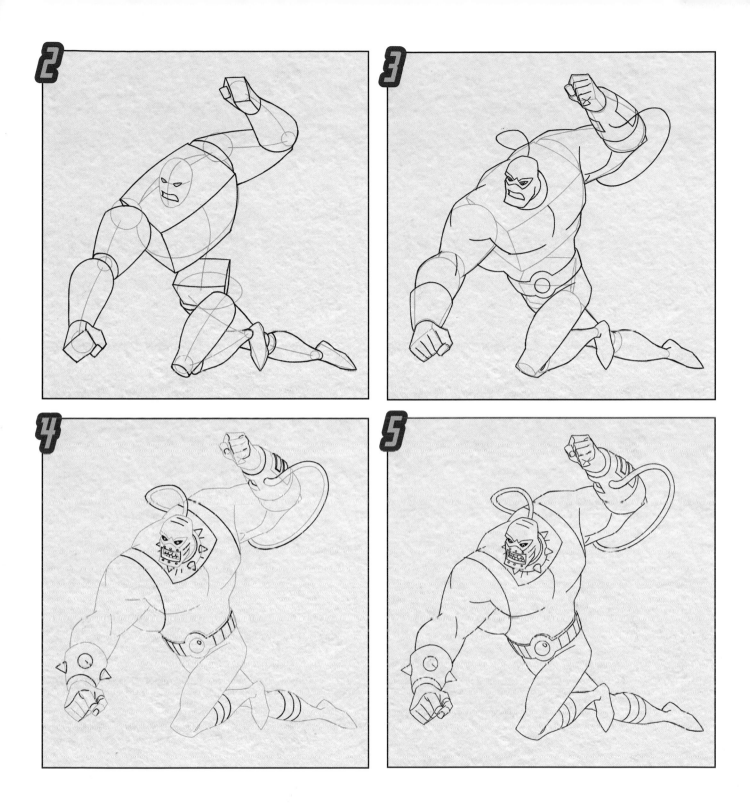

DRAWING IDEA

Try drawing Bane fighting with Batman on a bridge in Gotham City.

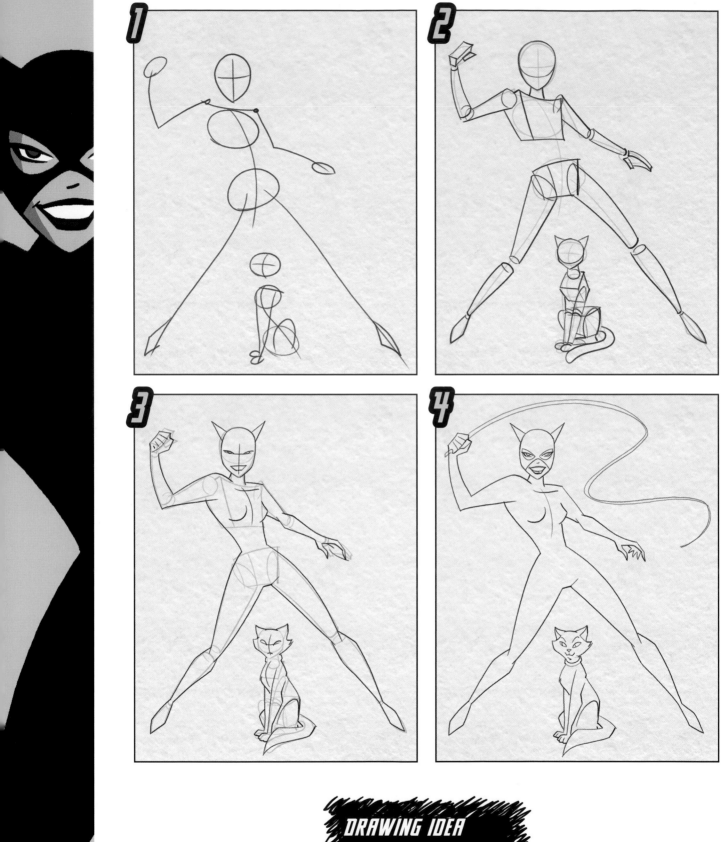

# CATWOMAN

Real Name: Selina Kyle

Home Base: Gotham City

Occupation: professional thief

Abilities: stealth, gymnastics and martial arts skills

Equipment: retractable claws

Background: Selina Kyle became an orphan at a young age. She grew up committing petty crimes to survive on the streets. Now as Catwoman, Selina is an incredibly stealthy and skilled burglar. She preys on Gotham City's wealthy citizens while protecting the city's less fortunate people. Selina has helped Batman to stop major criminals on several occasions. But their partnerships never last long. She has no interest in ending her own thieving ways.

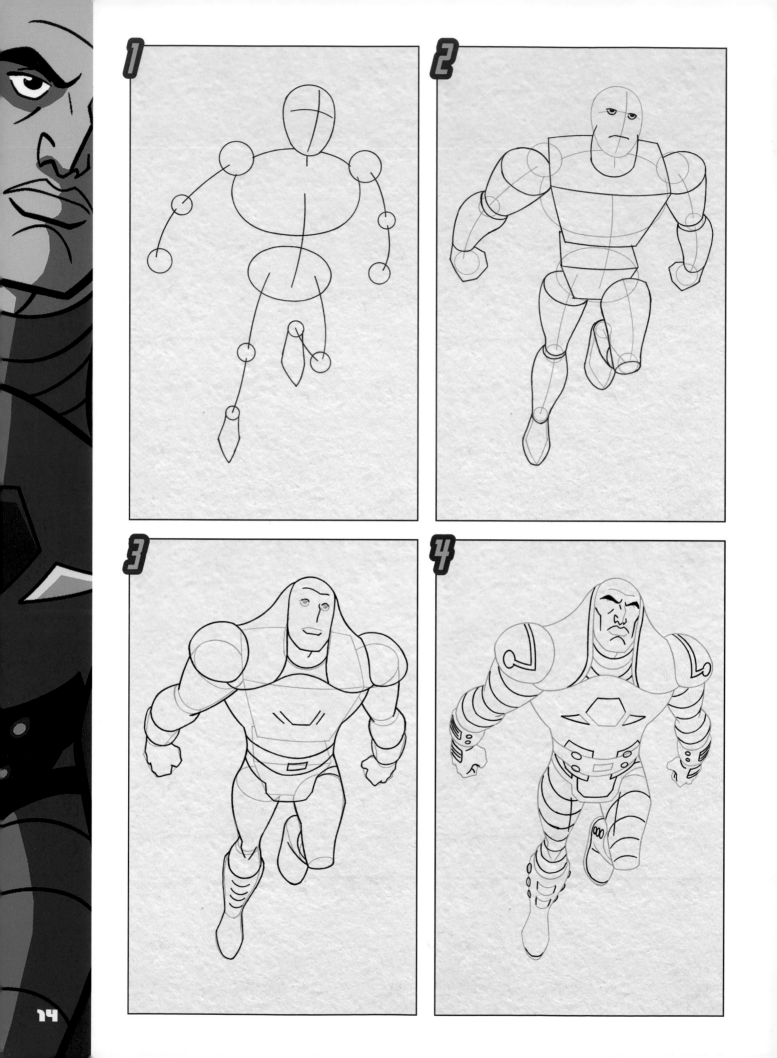

BATTLE ARMOUR LEX

Real Name: Lex Luthor

Home Base: LexCorp, Metropolis

Occupation: successful businessman, criminal mastermind

Enemy of: Superman

Abilities: scientific genius

Equipment: Kryptonite battle suit

DRAWING IDEA
Try drawing Lex battling Superman in his armour high over Metropolis!

Background: Lex Luthor is one of Metropolis' richest and most powerful people. Behind the scenes he is a criminal mastermind and a scientific genius. To deal with Superman, Lex built a Kryptonite-powered battle suit. The armoured suit gives him super-strength and allows him to fly. It's also armed with powerful Kryptonite energy weapons. While wearing his special battle suit, Lex is almost a match for Superman.

METALLO

Real Name: John Corben

Home Base: Metropolis

Occupation: criminal and super-villain

Enemy of: Superman

Abilities: enhanced strength and speed, metal transformation

Background: John Corben was a criminal who was once employed by Lex Luthor. While in prison, Luthor infected Corben with a deadly disease. To save himself, Corben agreed to an experimental medical procedure. But when he woke up, he discovered that his brain had been placed into a cyborg body powered by green Kryptonite. Now known as Metallo, he is nearly as strong and fast as Superman. The radiation from his Kryptonite heart is lethal to the Man of Steel.

DRAWING IDEA
Try drawing Metallo using his Kryptonite powers in a face-off against the Man of Steel!

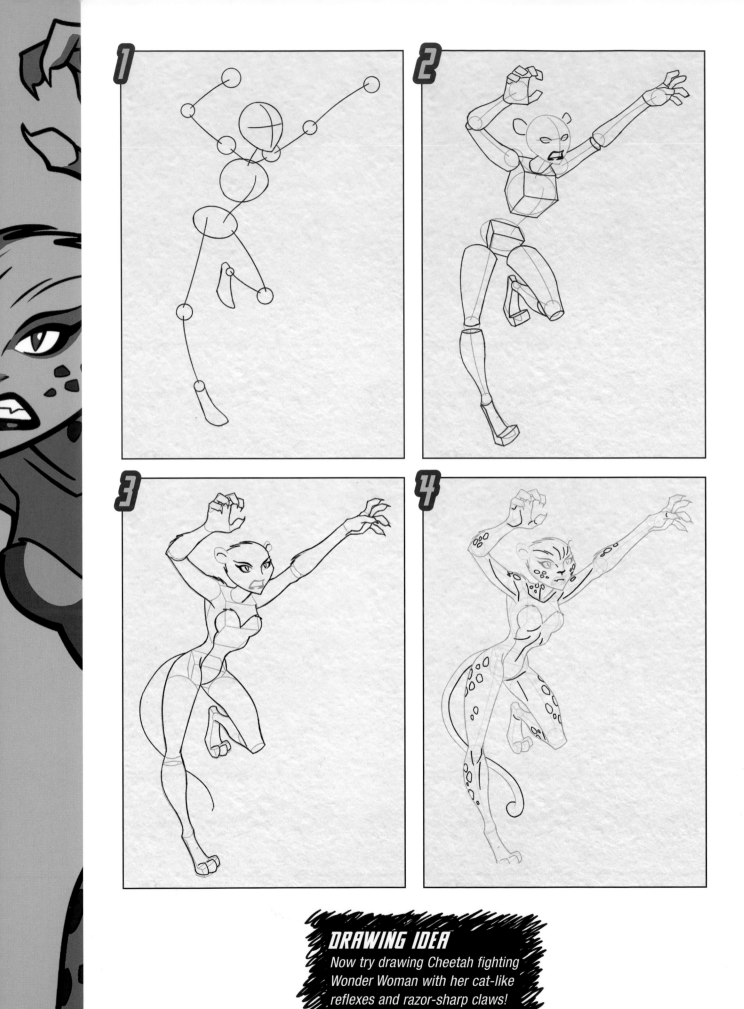

DRAWING IDEA
Now try drawing Cheetah fighting Wonder Woman with her cat-like reflexes and razor-sharp claws!

CHEETAH

Real Name: Barbara Ann Minerva

Home Base: Nottingham, UK

Occupation: biologist, professional criminal

Enemy of: Wonder Woman

Abilities: cat-like agility and reflexes, enhanced strength and speed, night vision, razor-sharp claws

Background: Dr. Barbara Ann Minerva was a biologist working on advanced genetics research. One day, she decided to test her research on herself. She was transformed into a half-human, half-cheetah hybrid. She was soon considered a freak by her fellow scientists and others. Cheetah then turned to a life of crime. She is cunning and clever, and her cat-like abilities make her a dangerous foe for Wonder Woman.

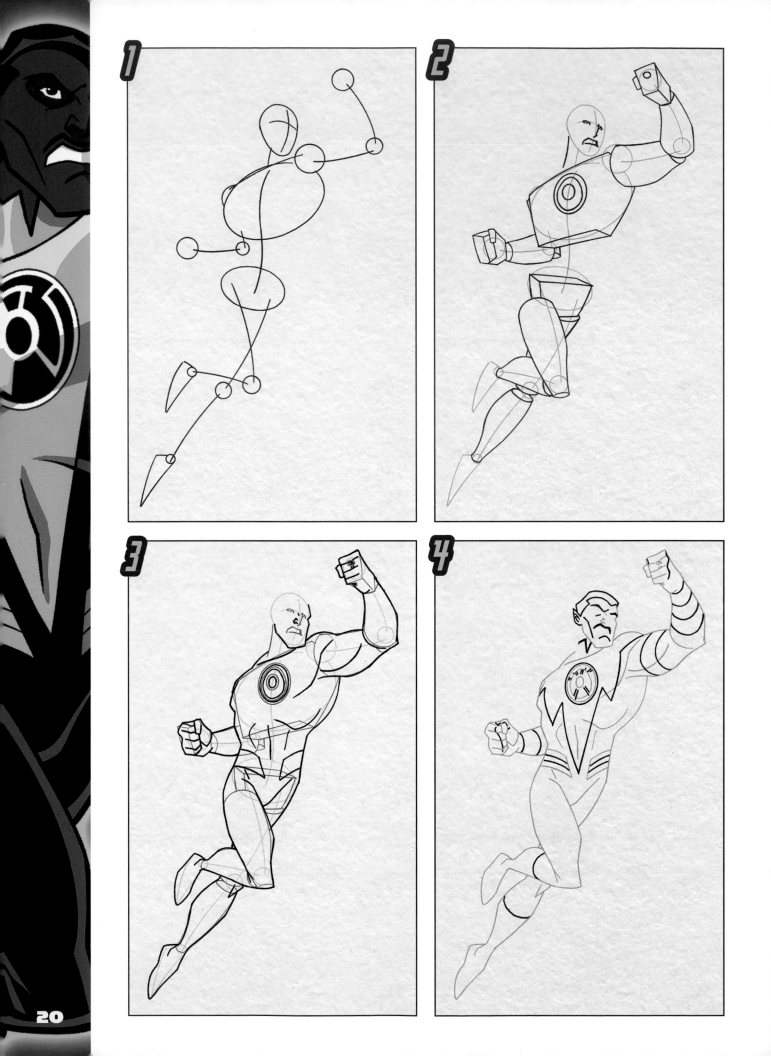

SINESTRO

Real Name: Thaal Sinestro

Home Base: Korugar, Qward

Occupation: Yellow Lantern

Enemy of: Green Lantern Corps

Abilities: military command, hand-to-hand combat skills, genius intellect

Equipment: yellow power ring

Background: Originally from the planet Korugar, Thaal Sinestro was once a famous member of the Green Lantern Corps. But he later turned to evil and became a dictator over his home planet. Sinestro was eventually captured and banished to the planet Qward. However, he later obtained a yellow power ring that was just as powerful as the Lanterns' green rings. Sinestro then formed the Sinestro Corps and swore to get his revenge against the Green Lanterns.

DRAWING IDEA
Next try drawing Sinestro creating a powerful weapon with his yellow ring to fight Green Lantern!

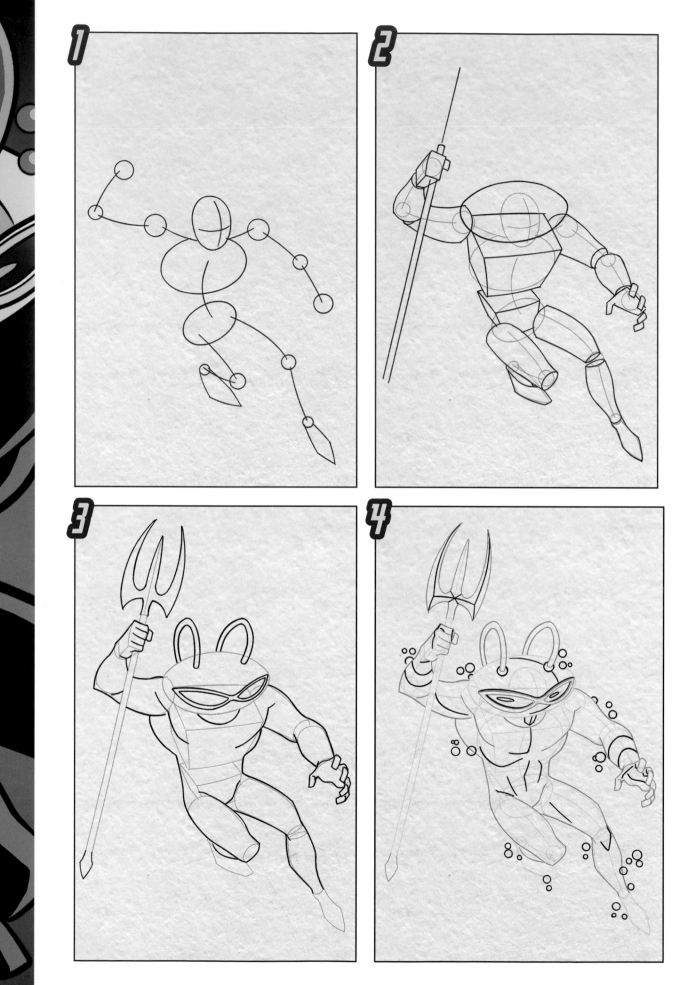

BLACK MANTA

Real Name: unknown

Home Base: the Ocean

Occupation: treasure hunter, assassin

Enemy of: Aquaman

Abilities: above-average strength and speed

Equipment: advanced diving suit, jet boots, miniature torpedoes, power helmet with infrared vision and energy beams

Background: As a young boy Black Manta was kidnapped and imprisoned on a small ship. One day, he saw Aquaman and called out for help, but the Sea King didn't hear him. At that moment the boy swore to get revenge on Aquaman. When he finally escaped, he designed a high-tech diving suit and helmet. Now Black Manta has two goals — to destroy Aquaman and to become ruler of the seas.

DRAWING IDEA
Try drawing Black Manta in an underwater fight with Aquaman and his sea creature friends!

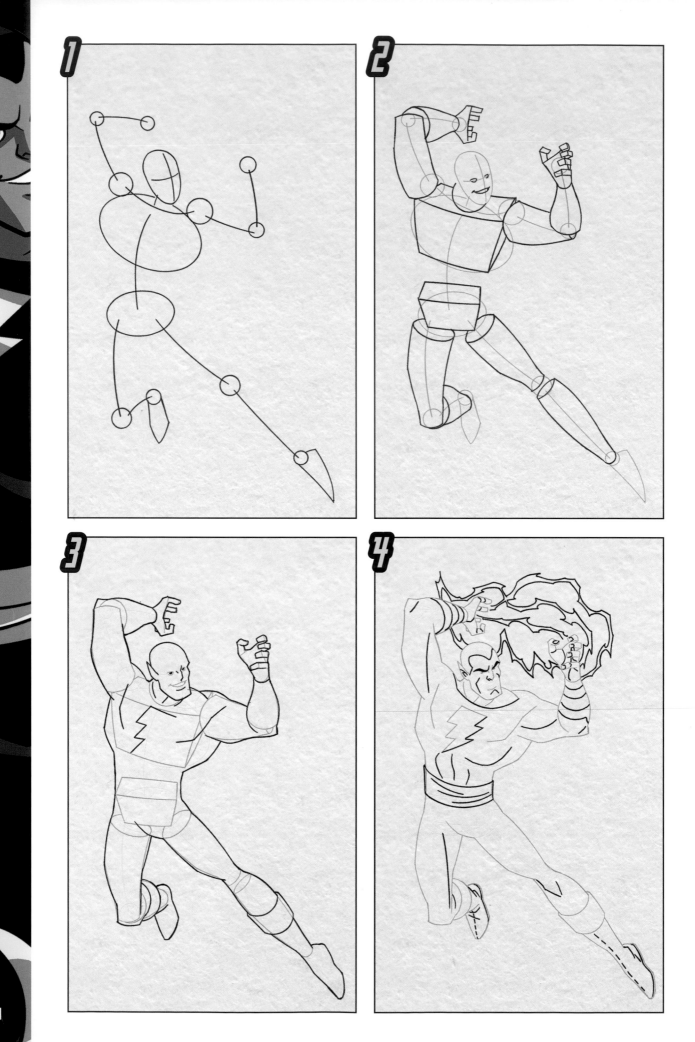

BLACK ADAM

Real Name: Teth-Adam

Home Base: Kahndaq

Occupation: dictator

Enemy of: SHAZAM!

Abilities: superhuman strength, speed and stamina; enhanced intelligence; accelerated healing; flight; invulnerability

DRAWING IDEA
Try drawing Black Adam using his magical powers to battle his arch-enemy SHAZAM!

Background: Teth-Adam was once a fair and honest prince. The wizard Shazam gave him the powers of the gods Shu, Heru, Amon, Zehuti, Aton and Mehen. But Adam later became a cruel dictator. Eventually, the wizard trapped Adam's soul and powers inside a magic necklace. However, the necklace was later discovered by Adam's descendant, Theo Adam. Now Black Adam's powers and memories live on through Theo. Only SHAZAM! can stop the super-villain's goal of ruling the world.

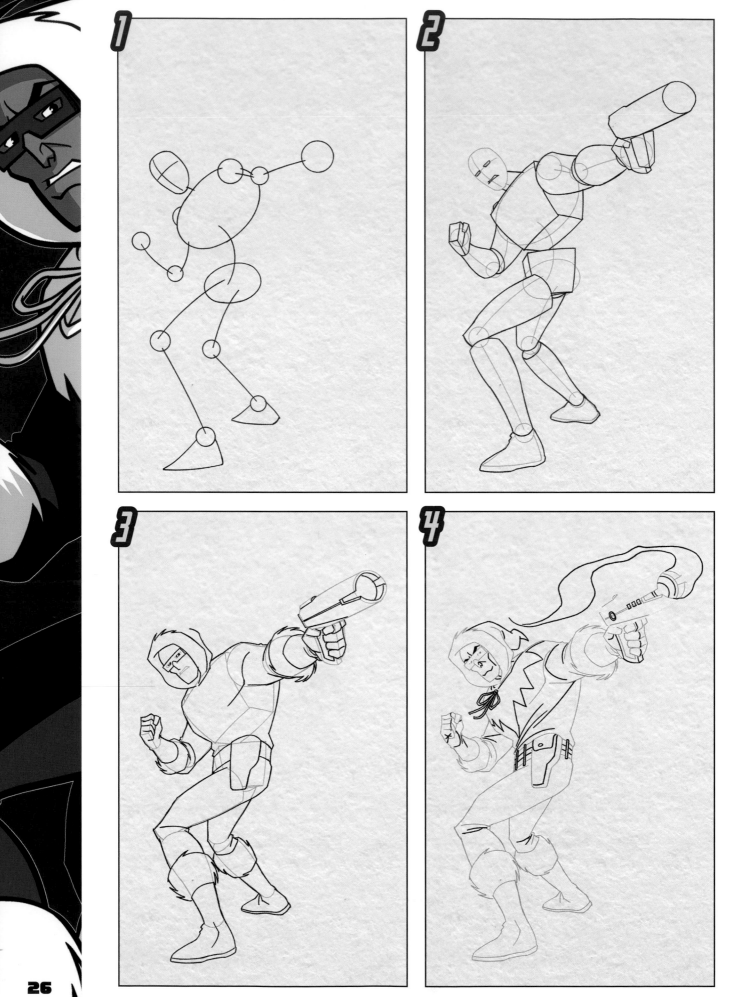

DRAWING IDEA
Now draw Captain Cold trying to blast The Flash with his powerful ultra-cold cannon!

CAPTAIN COLD

Real Name: Leonard Snart

Home Base: Central City

Occupation: professional criminal

Enemy of: The Flash

Abilities: skilled marksman, excellent strategist

Equipment: cold gun

Background: Captain Cold's name suits him well. He has nerves of ice and his cold heart helps him to stay cool and collected in any situation. His special cold gun can instantly freeze objects into solid ice. Captain Cold also created an ultra-cold cannon that can bring even The Flash to a standstill. Now he looks for his chance to put the Scarlet Speedster on ice for good!

SUPER-VILLAINS UNITED

Super-villains usually like to work alone. However, being a successful criminal can be difficult with super heroes around. To gain an advantage, villains sometimes form secret groups to fight their enemies together. These groups have had several names including the Secret Society of Super-Villains, the Injustice League and the Legion of Doom. Villains can be powerful and dangerous when they team up. But luckily, villains have a fatal flaw — they usually don't work well together. They often end up fighting with each other instead of the heroes they hate!

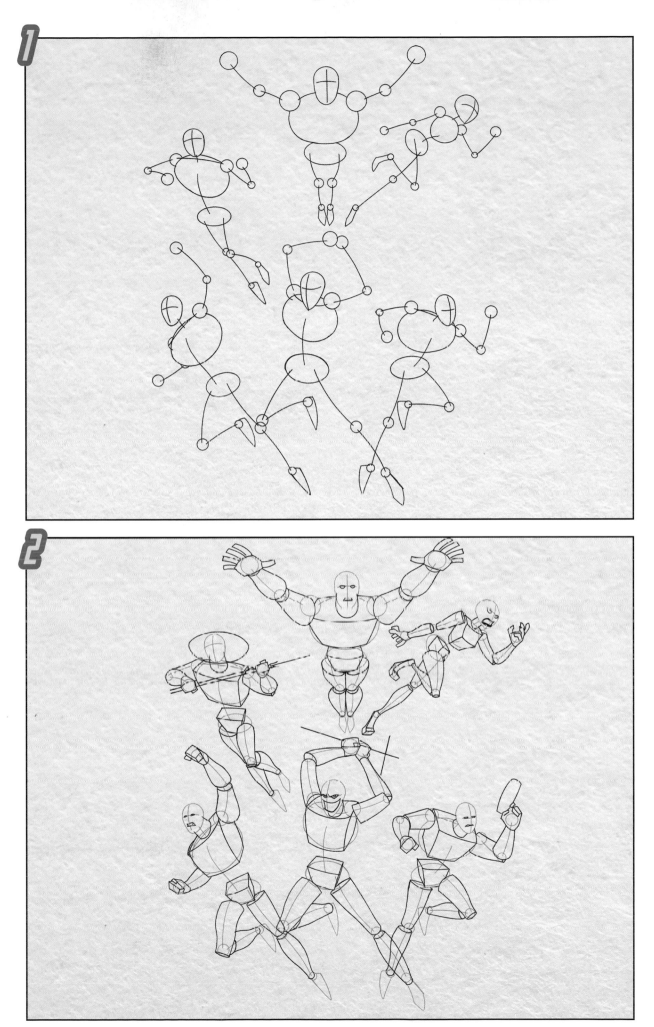

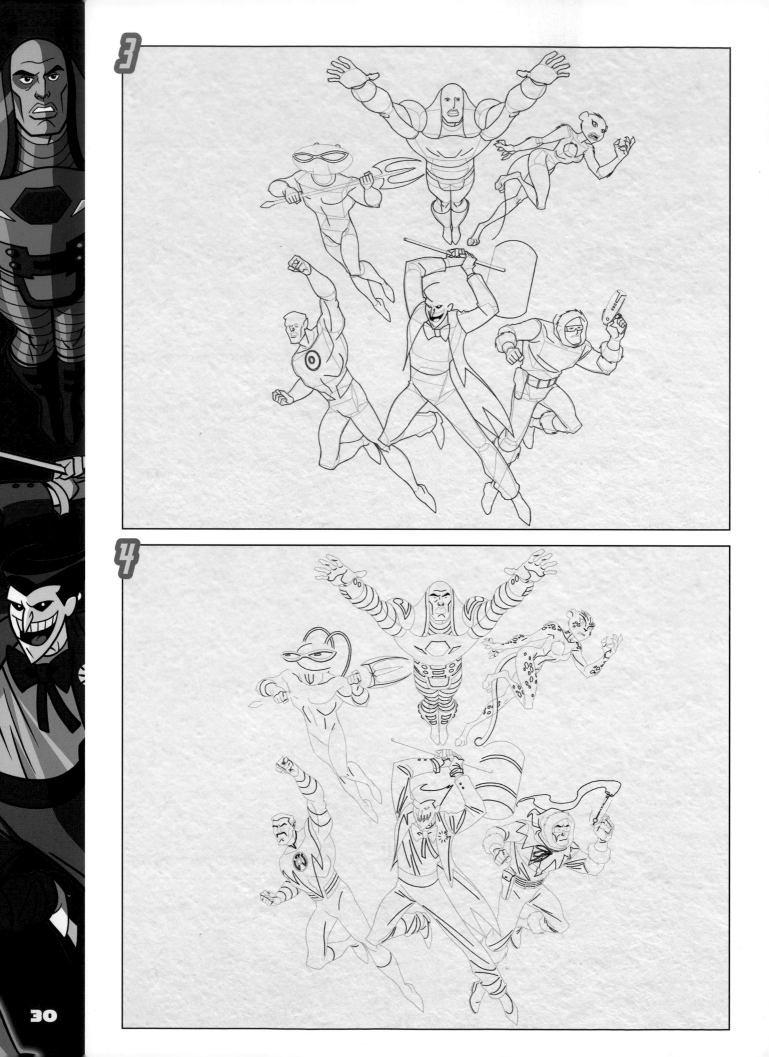

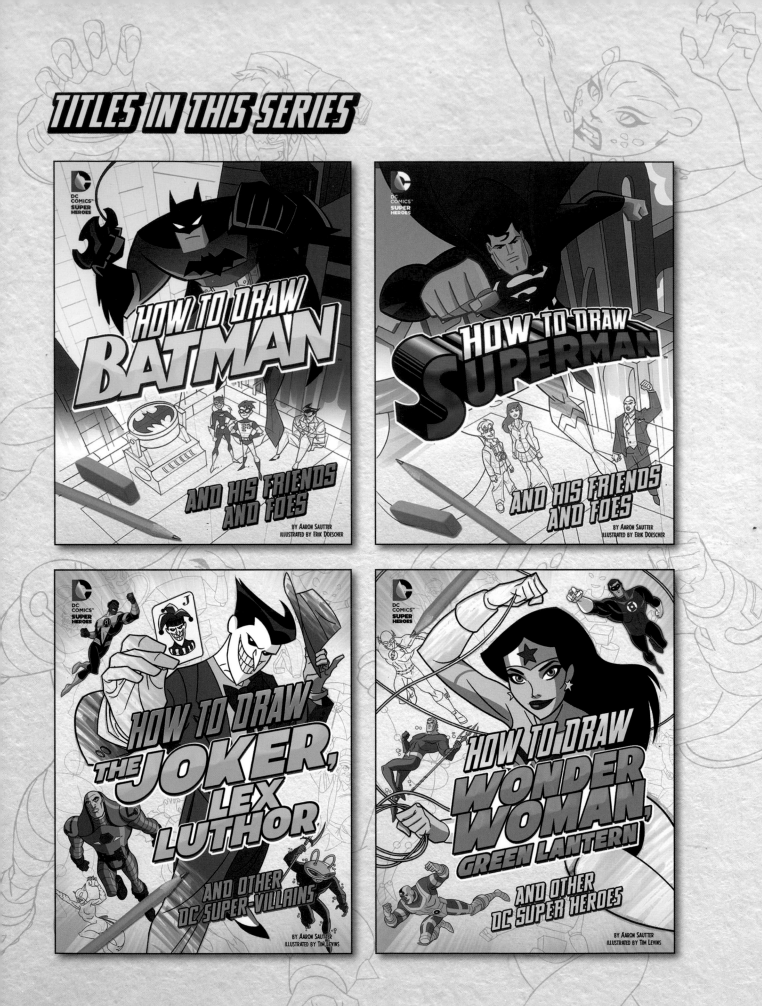